INSTAPOET

Augie's Bookshelf

INSTAPOET

INSTAPOET

© 2020 Augie's Bookshelf All rights reserved.

Published by: Augie's Bookshelf

Text Design by: Molly Wolchansky

A CIP record for this book is available from the Library of Congress Cataloging-in-Publication Data

Printed and bound in The United States

ISBN 9798622131240

Thank you to all of the amazing poets we found through the Instagram platform. You are incredible human beings.

#instapoetbook

I want someone to look at me and see
Inhabitable ground. I want them to see dirt
And roots and rivers and cliffs.
I want them to see salvation. I want to be
A saving grace. A call from the void
Of cataclysmic tragedies, whispering
Pleasantries and possibilities. I'm a temptation
That someone can cradle within rough hands
While tending to a kind heart. Look at me and see
Everything that I am not.

No one is an untouched gate to sanctitude,
There's destruction and live wires behind a façade
Of visional bodies. Taste grit and bury yourself
Into someone else's holy place.
The only ones that are truly otherworldly
Are the ones you don't know anything about.
Learn a place,
A name, a feeling, a face,
And you've already burned it down.

Finding Someone Else's Happy Place
@poetshy.w

You tuck my star-combed hair behind my ear

As dark-bodied cicadas call out to us this mid-summer sunset.

You whisper about that time you touched an empty God;

Awestruck and proud as it turned your hands silver.

I'll never tell you that the true color of holiness is golden,

Shimmering,

Dancing between divinity,

And my own Godliness

Ichor bleeds from my split lip,

But you don't seem to notice.

You'll only ever bleed like the fellow fallen,

Deep cherry wine from your nose,

And we both seem to notice.

The Perceptive Always Win

@poetshy.w

I'm eyeing combustion.
Its shadow walking
Its way into my head.
I never knew that loneliness
Could be a dagger in the belly.
I never knew that all along,
I was the one twisting it.

Where the Monsters Go to Hide
@poetshy.w

i wrote of you

like love tumbled from my breast

poured from my lips

all sweet and thick

your taste still inside my mouth

sticky and hot

making it hard to breathe anything but you

you

@j.maye_

you can't be the victim and the victor
silently sitting on the sidelines of your own life
wondering why you're invisible
you have to stand in the gap
between who you are and
who you've created yourself to be
(again and again)
i will no longer shrink
mold myself to be worthy of love and acceptance
I was born worthy

worthy
@j.maye_

the same mouth that kisses

also

bites

mouths

@j.maye_

the storm is coming & / i wrap my arms around the things i am afraid to
lose / the grizzled trees / the magnolia heart lines / their creamy petals /
the lavender garden / the chrysanthemums—

"please stay"— i whisper to their roots

"be still"— they whisper back

let these muddy prayers be enough / because i don't always know where
to put the sadness / it splits my pockets & falls into the dirt / hope is
messy here, smeared into the mud / but it's a fighter, too / it wriggles
from all the empty spaces / from the places we have wept / the things we
have lost / restoration will come with the clouds / we will put the flowers

in our hair again &

all we have lost

all we have lost

let it all return to us

@annesparow

open the

window &

let the morning

crawl inside

feel its mercies

kiss your skin

& its wings brush

along your collarbones

watch it grow wildflowers

from the soles

of your shoes

this light—

it's for you

open the window

let it in

@annesparow

grief sits in a chair

on the other side of the room

her hands shake & so do mine

our eyelids rimmed with fire & salt

grief reaches for my palms

opens the curtains

tucks the light behind my ear

she sits with me for the night

i am not sure how long it takes for me to look out the window

to see an egret soar in the sky

snow falling on a twilight sun

the wild birds promise to

sing at dawn

tell us that they too

have made it through

the night

@annesparow

I want to sit on the edge of the ocean
and let the sand run through my fingers.
I want my breath to catch the winds of waves
so I can exhale the belief that I am lacking
as they console me and encourage me to
aim higher.

@amoriepoetry

This day is so silent
but my thoughts are so loud.
They are asking me how
I let you get away.
This is a question that I
cannot seem to answer.

This day is so lovely
but my heart is so heavy.
It is asking me if the ache
of your absence will ever subside.
This is a question that I can answer.
No, my heart, it will not.

This day is one that I chose.

This Day
@amoriepoetry

To which my soul succumbs to pain--
The heart moves in its decadent way
How many times can I struggle relentlessly?
I'm weary and tired, if only someone would see
The abyss grows deeper and deeper every waking hour
Like my screams cannot be heard by another
Hoping that light will invade the shadows within
Chase away these ruthless demons
Do not rest, for they will win
They thirst for life as they are hollow
They are like a depleted desert;
Room to grow, but no nourishment there

To Which My Soul
@amoriepoetry

I have admired so many people
as if they were works of art—
down to every crooked tooth,
dark circle, and faded scar
Each curve, each perfectly
or imperfectly placed strand of hair

One day I discovered I could
look at myself in the same way
Each familiar part of me appearing
as strange and uniquely beautiful
to the eyes of another as they
appeared in mine

So I stepped outside and
became the stranger,
appreciating the parts of me
I once had been too close
to recognize

@marissabeste

The more I wander, the more I am lost
Not hopelessly lost, but a free lost
One where nothing belongs to me,
instead everything does

The creeks, the doves, the black bears
they are friends and family
Any place I rest my head is home
Even if it's a patch of grass or a window pane

Speak to me like I'm family, skip
the pleasantries and tell me where
you came from, where we all are from

I am too connected in meaningless ways
Show me ways to care that are genuine and vintage
Teach this new dog some old tricks

I am wise in useless ways—
remind me that I know nothing

@marissabeste

I daydreamed, ankles crossed,
on scratchy carpet and biting crab grass,
tasting sweet melons and ripe tomatoes

I opened toy boxes filled with satin dresses
and plastic dolls, wooden windows open
and rain streaming down the gutters

Rain in the summer, what a pleasant
spectacle, when thunder rumbled in
and birds sang on despite darkening,
swirling clouds and buzzing green foliage

I prayed for tornadoes to sneak up
and swirl me away, run me across
the fields and drop me in another land

Drape me over rafters in someone's
old barn, or I'll land in the middle of a forest
with running streams and large spiders

When I woke up, I was in an ocean
colored deep crimson, floating on stacks
of books and covered in a patchwork quilt

@marissabeste

My mother carried a candid picture of my father
Standing in a desert
Sun hitting just right
Smiling effortlessly
Before this world would make him forget how

This was the photo of the man she was to wed
This was the photo she kept
Under her pillow every night
Hoping to dream of the new life she was to have

My father carried a posed picture of my mother
Braided pleat down to her waist
Smile just wide enough but not too much
Coconut trees swaying in the background
Reminding him of the life he had left behind

This was the photo of the woman he was to wed
This was the photo he kept
Tucked between the folds of his wallet
Always a finger lengths away
To remind him of the new life he was to have

To say my parents shared an epic romance would be a lie
But they built a life out of silent pictures and short phone calls
Fostered respect before there was ever love

I wonder
When they stopped being strangers sharing a bed
When they became friends
If they ever became lovers
If they share a secret love story they never told us

If staying together was a decision of choice

Or one for which they saw no alternative because it was all they had ever known

When asked about my father

My mother will always name

All of the ways in which he has provided a good life

All of the ways he is a good father

When asked about my mother

My father will always name

All of the ways she has been a good partner

Fulfilling all of the duties of both wife and mother

But my parents never spoke of

How it felt when they first met

Or how it felt when their eyes met for the first time

Or of any firsts

Or feelings really

Their love looked so different

Than the one I always envisioned for myself

See, their love was rooted in something different all together

Rooted in desire

But not for each other

Rather

To survive

To make it in a world that wasn't built for them

To build a life on hostile ground

No matter the cost

So, who am I to not call their love epic?

27

@ribtobeyond

the problem with making a home out of a person is
when he leaves you are left homeless
caught in a storm of your own making
because you let your roof be made of flawed human

when you make the four walls of your home
the four limbs of another damaged soul
should you be surprised the foundation is faulty?

when you make your fireplace
the warmth of his chest
should you be surprised at the chills when he is no longer there?

see homes weren't supposed to be in the arms of another person
because arms can only hold so much without failing

i guess that's why homes shouldn't be made of people
because we
see, we are flawed by design

@ribtobeyond

We're all trying to survive in a world of possibilities,

Each of us carrying the truth.

Mine is light,

Shining from droplets of water caught by the hairs on my body as I bask
in the sun.

Your truth is warped,

Like the wood of the tree you fell.

Trapped under, you lay, you lie, lost under the weight of your words.

My sympathy set with the sun but won't rise again.

For where I built fires to keep us warm,

You claim I burnt you.

You greedily ate my nourishment,

But vowed that you spat me out.

I led you to water where you drank,

But told of drowning.

From now on,

Plant your poison elsewhere.

This is my land and here,

My woes wilt, not my flowers.

Alive, I Thrive
@the.free.words.of.me

The hot water cradles our want.

Naked skin pressed on a stolen afternoon,
Seconds tied in wishes of forever,
Soft sunlight is drawn to your happy eyes
They cry 'meet me halfway, let this be always'
In a foreign bath that never felt such heat
At any time, in any weather.

I search for sentiments that bind.

Longing for you to hold words for longer
Than you can hold me now,
Sticking past the slow rolls of oil down your beating chest,
Find my sweet truths, unsold and then
Permit them to cling, let them linger and rest
When I can't be near to stress how I adore you.

My fibres glisten in your sight.

Contoured backs reflect in misted glass,
We listen as wills sink down a struggling plug,
Just one more night, that's all I ask,
Worries washed and good love pouring from pores,
The bliss of smoothing your every arch,
Imagine more afternoons passing like this.

A Sunlit Afternoon Bath
@the.free.words.of.me

Should we never meet again, tell her to live like the wind.

Boundless, free and unapologetic

To force through cloudy days and haunt the nights with howling laughs,

teasing midnight blues from the tawny owl's claw

To rule both soft and hard, breathing through June's pink peonies and

blasting the rocky mountain tops, however high

To carry the wings of those she loves. Even when they wish to wander far

to unfamiliar senses; different, disgusting and delicious

To be forever wild, permitting her inner child to make mischief on busy

city streets, tossing umbrellas and squinting eyes

To spread her stories, memories and moments like dandelion seeds.

They may not be the prettiest, but we learn from our roots

And lastly, to never, ever dwell. Whatever the weather, rush the shadows

and give them hell.

Like the Wind

@the.free.words.of.me

I think of you sometimes
and your last apology
still feels like sharp bone
fragments in my mouth;
out of place and
impossible to swallow

I think of you sometimes
and I try to crush the remnants
between my teeth
but each time, I fear they will crush me
and I hope, one day, I'll spit them out
and learn acceptance through living
but right now, I taste blood from
forcing my tongue to be forgiving

I think of you sometimes
and you remind me that
what holds us together can
weaken and crack,
how the past can become a foreign land
and how a stranger, once a friend,
can become a stranger again

Stranger
@susurruspoetry

I must remember to be thankful
for bird songs and
the inquisitive manner of dogs' noses
and the way old trees creak when
the wind asks them to dance
and the way cat ears move
when greeting life's music
and the way mustard seeds
move mountains
and the way our roots,
though buried deep below,
ultimately lead to our
unfurling and reaching and
the way a tiny pinch of hope
can convince us to rise
again and again

Thankful
@susurruspoetry

I sit and wait

in a state of subtle disquiet

and the air moves

heavily and silently around me

as though time itself

has conspired against me

and a clock somewhere

in the room says tick

and I hear

another second gone

and then it says tock

and I think

another second wasted

But no;

this transitional time has purpose,

there is no waste in this waiting

Waiting

@susurruspoetry

The book of me and all I am
is dusted off and open for you
to discover, read, and learn

but I believe I've made a mistake
because you only flip through
carelessly skimming my pages

so please, set me down easily
close me back up and walk away
I now remember why
I've kept myself this way

@ashleynicolepoetry

Just love me fiercely
so that the cold within
burns from passion
and melts away
so I can simply forget
the numbing of the frost
that left me disabled
to begin with

@ashleynicolepoetry

I am a ship in a bottle
dreaming of navigating open waters
and feeling the salty air through my sails
yet this glass contains me
and I am unable to break free

@ashleynicolepoetry

These strings of starlight

Are spinning new constellations

As I untangle

The high strung sky

And they stagger

Littered through time

Watching the moon

Sing lullabies to the

Sleeping Earth below

And I wait in your shadow

Clinging onto the brightest star

I can find

(Can I be a star too?)

@taylorlutkapoetry

You had my heart in your hand
And my soul in your back pocket
And you carried me around
Like a deck of cards
Waiting to show someone your tricks
You had the slight of hand
That disappeared into the gaps
Carved in my skin
And pulled on the strings of stars
Etched along the edges of my silhouette
You knew where to grab along my tired facade
To make starlight in yourself
And you carried me around like a trophy
The only little pocket of sunshine
You'd need.
(You stole the pieces that made me, me)

@taylorlutkapoetry

Just like the wings

Of a hummingbird

Cannot be seen,

I was transfixed

By the feeling

And lost

In the mirage

(and you were just as fleeting)

@taylorlutkapoetry

She strums Autumn between her nostalgic fingers humming at the rubs of sweater strands; sings truth to the realm of courage. She is an old polaroid suspended by jute string where she has become an heirloom of brave. She is unusual, the flower behind the wall. Bruised amber for a crown that only a few can perceive. Soon you will reckon with her for she is bubbling complete. She is the root, the tree, and everything after.

She is September Girl.

September Girl
@theimpossiblewriter

An empty grave comes in the shapeshifter of unbelief ravenous to swallow new beginnings and bury each of them alive. It is when our reveries become sonnets upon large napkins that are lost in diner booths. Leave her the tip; get the dirt under your nails and don't let this be your October.

October
@theimpossiblewriter

I exit left as I remove the coat of unworthiness, leaving him strangled and bleeding at center stage. I withdraw myself into the wave of the grande drape as my frame trembles confronting the memories of the one who plotted to inhale my rag doll innocence. I weave my way through the absence of light, unrelenting. I chew the amber warmth and it coats my throat with spontaneous victory. It also cuts inebriation like a knife; thrusting soberness of thinking as these words conceive my freedom. "This is your sign dear one, and you will not perish. You will breathe a story of a prevailing life of how you discerned the exit signs from the monsters that are called lies.

Exit Signs
@theimpossiblewriter

Are we even meant to meet?
Are we even meant to speak?
When the two of us are different
From where we are and where we've been
Up at the north you flourish with your winter
I'm at my east with all the falling leaves and summer

I'll dream of us, day and night
Where we can meet, and it'll feel right
Where metal stitches brought us face to face
And I shall thank the Heavens for such grace
But nay, I have done acts of villainy
I do not deserve this, even as a fantasy

Axis

@odesofartisan

Your dreams can take you places, or it will take you home. Either way, you'll find happiness right where you belong. Be assured, beloved, that this is the work of the universe. Such an odd thing of an odd thinking, creating art out of our lives, our happily ever afters are their masterpieces.

Constellation
@odesofartisan

I pray that she tells me. She tells me the secrets of the sun, or the language of the stars. What the moon whispers in the dark, or the conspiracies of the creatures, shadow and light. I pray for her to tell me how they all made you so celestial and yet so wonted. How they have woven your soul to be perfection and yet question its own purpose when it defines you.

Letter to the Universe
@odesofartisan

you threw the ring
into the lake
beside your house
as i held a match
to our favorite picture of us
and it was a long time ago
that we decided to
drown
and burn
each other
but sometimes
i wonder
if you still choke on
the smoke
the same way i often
forget how
to breathe.

lungs
@k.t.decker_poetry

i wonder

if mailmen

notice

and feel sad

when people send letters

to one another

less and less

until eventually

they just stop

altogether.

postage
@k.t.decker_poetry

to heal
will be impossible
without forgiveness
of both
others
and
self.

beginnings
@k.t.decker_poetry

i have experienced
so many beginnings
that i did not recognize
at the time
as new stages of life
for we seem to fall into
foreign patterns
as easily as colored glass
falls through a kaleidoscope
and become different people
in the span of a few heartbeats
from all the colorful conceptions
that define us.

spectrums
@k.t.decker_poetry

She took off those last layers, and tossed them to the floor. Her soul felt as tired as the earthen vessel that contained it. She climbed into that warm cocoon, a much needed respite from the pain. It embraced her spirit lovingly, and wouldn't let go until she was new again.

@lady_introverted

You will outgrow that place, that place inside of you where you keep everything safely tucked away. Dreams can only live so long when they are preserved in perfection. Sooner or later, they need to leave the protection of the mind. Sooner or later, those dreams need to be born.

@lady_introverted

Those knots, perfectly aligned along her spine, a divine sign that
she was never meant to carry the weight of the world.

@lady_introverted

I

first cut

first scar

first in line

first in love

first falling-out

first to forgive

first to move on:

the first child

II

like a buddha

grounded, cross-legged

sits the middle child:

unwavering calm

in the eye of a storm

III

the youngest child is left

the hand-me-downs:

though not shiny or new,

while broken in,

they have been well-loved

Siblings

@petite.sprout

The wind will move on, one day,
and take with it discarded
bark and loosened leaves.
Bird wings. Stark husks
and forest seeds.
Leaving only a bitter chill.
Till spring.
Our bed, that night, was ice.
Cold. Forbidding.
I cleaved the sheets.
Couldn't bear to lie there.
Empty, as it were.
Spread out.
A vast plain of nothing.
Perverse, without meaning.
Barely animate. Hidden.
Since you left.

Since

@petite.sprout

At the beginning, one's fingernails smell of the earth, the wind ties knots of rebellious strands, and all seems possible. The world, ragged and boundless, seen through mist-tinted eyes, tastes like a dream. Later may come thorns, may come eggshells, may fracture and herald a season of shards. As life gets harder, so may our hearts. But there, at the start of our timeline, still remains life's elixir — softness of soul, the truths of beauty and wonder — patiently awaiting reunion, ready to quench parched lips with its succour.

how I learned to count:
two feet, one path, zero eggshells
pricking a tender sole

Roaming
@petite.sprout

at day's close

i am the keeper

    of the grove

the silence

     of the arbour

  my night

sinks into the down

  of your leaves

  and grows darker

     at your centre

you are sublime

     dreams

  planted

  in sleep

breathless

    by morning

 i awake in your dawn

foliage flayed

  musk stippling

  i seek protection

in your

  sealing

i plant a forest at your feet

@petite.sprout

When you left,
I fell to pieces,
like snowflakes falling
from the wintery
night sky,
reflecting the
world around me,
knowing I would
melt without you.

@etc.poet

When I am too weary
to even hold a thought,
your spirit reaches
down and lifts me
from my burdens for
just a moment, long
enough for me to catch
my breath and sense that
I am still loved, from afar...
and all is softened.

@etc.poet

He adored her for the sunshine and
pleasantries she brought to the world,
sprinkling rose petals in her path,
but little did he know, she ascended
mountains, leaped from cliffs, trekked
through forests with beasts of the night,
marking her path with boots of steel
and strides of vigor...for she was not
a delicate flower, she was a boulder,
channeling a course of anything but
sunshine and pleasantries.

@etc.poet

I know you are floundering,
a little, then a lot...
You are frustrated and tired,
disheartened and distraught.
You lost sight of your dreams,
you're reaching for a raft.
One event has led to the next,
white caps are pulling you back.
It takes intention and strength
to swim against the stream.
The river flows fast and strong,
not in line with your dreams.
You settle to keep up,
it's okay, I do too.
I am still in this world,
always, always for you.

@etc.poet

I often get asked

"Where do you live?"

It is my favourite question

I live in an effervescent garden

Of flowers

Who grow as tall as the highest trees

I bathe in the sweet nectar of my body

Where every word is kind

And every touch is gentle

"Don't you ever wonder where they live?"

Is the question that always follows

As if I would ever want to leave

Or question

What was given to me

What was crafted for me

My temple is a place

That no one else can replicate

That others can only dream of

- I am home

Home

@_soulpoems

Pain will come

And when it does

You will be swept up

In its tidal wave

Its tenacity

Will penetrate through

Your bones

Don't resist my darling

This pain is teaching you

Sculpting you

Feel it

Let it swallow you

Whole

- This is the only way you move forward

The Essence of Pain

@_soulpoems

You will go on

To live

A horribly

Miserable life

If you continue

To plant your roots

And your worth

In someone else's

Garden

The Garden
@_soulpoems

Sometimes life will be so
Heavy
That you will feel a perpetual ache
All over your body
Your limbs will feel the weight
Of a hundred mountains
You may notice all of the
Little cracks and broken pieces
Floating inside of you
They are contributing
To the lack of normalcy
Within you
Sit with this
Hold it
Make room for it
Sometimes all you can do
Is accept that whatever you feel
Is just how you feel at this time
And it is never
Your permanent state
Of being

The Weight of Life
@_soulpoems

I am the space in the centre of e v e r y t h i n g.

I'm every misfit, every weird kid,

the secluded, reclusive with the loudest heartbeat in the room kid

-cut any background noise, I don't need a beat-

you don't need to hear me, see me, simply feel me...

I best exist in the silence

(why I'm beneath your skin screaming)

and within the spaces which unite us.

We are the matter in the n o t h i n g n e s s.

We are war cry sounded in interconnected heartstrings.

@cicerofocus

She, a healer who forgets she too deserves healing.
She, who has convinced herself she can love in a language
making even Lucifer sound angelic,
a human still beautifully clueless that her vocals far surpass
his dehumanising didactic;
yet she is who eagerly waits window seat pained for retribution of her
efforts.
(She still confuses reward with punishment,
and that valuing her is actually an act that is effortless.)
But she, who leaves the blinds open just enough
-(I see the truth that is stained)-
unsuccessfully masks her inner crusade
regardless of how many times she's tried looking away.
(She's yet to realise blinds do not hide the same, shade the shame, like a
blind eye)
This magnificent red carpet written within fairytales
is powered by the powder of done and dusted demons
which have been tucked underneath it;
(she is the beauty in the beast and this cellar is far from a castle.)
Would she trust the new dawn that is my palm,
a sun that doesn't rise and isn't the shade of violet?
Take my hand...
(I already know your pulse is racing to begin again.)

@cicerofocus

She is the kind of woman you want to wrap inside of an empire.

@cicerofocus

Early morning, winter cold or summer breeze,

a hot cup full and it warms my heart with ease.

Bitter alone but sweet in flavour,

just add sugar, honey, maple, whatever.

Smooth as butter with every sip I take,

no judgements as I surrender to its cordial embrace.

A ritual with my hands and there you stand,

an elixir of life to make the day less bland.

Coffee
@theramblingofamillennial

Tension, nerves, desperation.

Sight, movement, acceleration.

Ferocity, savage, victorious.

Hunger, nourished, glorious.

A bow, an arrow, a knife, a gun.

Life or death, the chase before the fall of the sun.

The Hunt

@theramblingofamillennial

Have you ever felt it?

A burning desire to take what is yours.

No care for the aftermath, the breakout of wars.

To claim absolute power in all its glory.

An adventure worth telling, written, a story.

Set a flame your path and sail the floods.

A legacy legendary paid in blood.

Cease to follow and aspire to be followed.

Gather all men to guard a lonely heart so hollow.

A conquerer with conquests, loves only in the night.

Savage once more and heirless come daylight.

King of the land, ruler of the flock, but all you left behind was a body to rot.

Your story will be told, studied and read.

But you will not be admired, for all things you left dead.

You're God

@theramblingofamillenial

You see those photos
of construction workers
taking lunch on steel beams
500 feet in the air,
or loggers letting their legs
hang from the severed top
of a Ponderosa.
You think Who would
be so crazy? I could
never do that.
And turn around to leap
into love, dangling by lips
speaking promises,
and sometimes you fall
without realizing you're
just a logger
harvesting forever.

Photos
@camden.m.jones

An empty casket borne

by a caisson draped in red and white

rattled through Philadelphia.

Twelve clergy,

disciples of a revolution,

single file having walked

the 155 miles from Mt. Vernon.

And in front –

two marines wearing black scarves

white gloves escorted a riderless horse

named Blueskin

who carried the general's

saddle, sabre, and pistols,

hollow boots reversed in stirrups

to look back at his country

on one final ride.

Nothing, not birdsong nor sobbing

broke the silence

except the rumble of the wagon

and the ring of hooves on stone

coming, then going.

If there were drums, the streets don't recall them.

What Philadelphia Saw at George Washington's Funeral Procession
@camden.m.jones

She says 'I am your truest love
And your most soul-shaking fear.'
She says 'I put the breath in your lungs
And salt in your tears.'
She sends gulls into the city
To cry my name over the
Train track screech.
She knows I need her peace.
The ocean is calling me.

To the Sea
@sol.et.luna.writes

If growth really
does conclude
pain perhaps
that's why I spent
a life of sunshine
searching for rain
pelted with
'sheltered' and
'too sensitive' for
crying storms under
the cloudless blues
but maybe I was
never trying to
bury myself,
maybe I wanted
simply to bloom.

Bloom
@sol.et.luna.writes

Give me nitty

gritty gravelly

ugly sandpaper

rough and ready

skin shedding

tugging at heartstrings

forehead kisses

catching on lip rings

hopeless 'sorry's'

worried worries

let us live

in this place

for eternity.

That Kind of Love

@sol.et.luna.writes

To this day I flinch
every time I hear a door slam
and breaths cease in my throat,
refusing to come out,
for the fear of reliving nightmares
that were real.
Where slamming doors turned into
windows smashed
graduating to punches thrown at walls
to then being pinned against them
unable to breathe.
Or move.

Men
who slam doors
are making sure you hear
their thoughts of how
instead of walls and dishes
they wish it was you.

I Heard it Loud and Clear
@uncagedbynavi

Closed doors don't stop

yelling

fighting

the shoving

or things being thrown.

Their sounds enter without invitations.

A closed door doesn't stop him from leaving

and the silence that follows announcing his departure

is louder than the breaking of dishes

and lost hope.

However closed doors

can

stop

from comforting those who are left

and those who seek comfort

from

picking up pieces of a broken home

never asking for help

with the hope it will survive yet another day.

Bandaged and Cracked
@uncagedbynavi

Falling in love with someone
seems easier than with
the reflection staring back in the mirror.
Uprooting my heart and handing it off
like an attention hungry beast
or a plant quenched for water
only satisfied by the actions and words of others.
How can I forget that I am just as important
and worthy of the love
I pour into others in abundance.
Patience is required to grow
and thrive
I must tend to my own garden
pull out the weeds of doubt because
I have affirmations to sow that
I do deserve it all.

Bloom
@uncagedbynavi

Your exit from my heart was no softly

closing door

It was the frantic chaos

of a midnight escape

under a moonless sky

running through the dark

scrambling over fences

sending sirens blaring

lights flashing and guns blazing

You left with the brute force

of battering rams and dynamite

exploding violently out of these bones

>Your exit was not the sweet goodbye
>
>of waves gently letting go of the shore
>
>It was the dark storm of bloody sorrow
>
>crashing against clenched teeth
>
>and flooding my eyes with rain

>Your exit was not the slow ripening
>
>of the sky at sunset
>
>gradually leading my heart into nightfall
>
>It was bricks hurled through
>
>stained glass windows
>
>spinning me into a kaleidoscope of
>
>jagged colorful edges

>Your exit from my heart
>
>left me shattered
>
>full of holes
>
>and cutting myself over and over
>
>on all these broken pieces

@breaking.golden

I will write
but not for you
I will bleed this ink
but these cuts are not yours
I will turn my heart inside out
but you do not get to lay claim to what's inside
and I will shape these ideas that I hold
not as sacrifices to your gods
but as wings to set me free from the bonds
of every expectation and
chain you have shackled to my feet
I write to set myself free

@breaking.golden

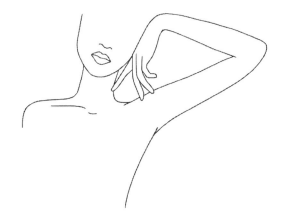

Dress me up with a few of your

pretty little lies

I do enjoy this game

Of costume change

As we banter back and forth

But, damnit

make sure you always strip me bare

with nothing but the truth to wear

@breaking.golden

Bright lights glinted off the metallic tide,
And oil slick rainbows reflected the mirage of fame.
We squeezed in like wrangled cattle, side by side,
Cheering for those who would never know our names.
Sharp shoes to pierce willing and fragile fates,
Plastic advertisements in the passing faces
For doctors who would smooth and sate.
No destinations but people were going places.
Credits roll remembering the ones waylaid
By broken promises and unreal stakes:
They shimmer and shine for a moment, then fade
To black when there is nothing left to take.

City of Dreams
@mmxxpoet

Sunlight blinds my eyes to even ordinary places
And sweet fantasy transforms to wastelands;
The words on the page morph into broken faces
Mocking my mortality as I drift through time's hands.
Each rising breath becomes an insurmountable peak,
Each clock's tick a perpetual reverberation,
As the heart pumps madly to continue its beat,
Stuck in the clutches of sick psyche's manipulation.
I lie down to commiserate with the fallen horizon
But I melt to black asphalt in a road to nowhere,
Yet the traffic of lost souls is fierce and rising
Like the tide of dreams that were never dared.

Mad Mind
@mmxxpoet

Our chosen leaders rose while we languished
With minds helpless and hearts famished,
Discarded after we chose a paper name:
One among many that were all the same.
Noble democracy bowed her head in defeat
While faithless capitalism pilfered her seat,
Twisting her values in his desire for power:
Among such weeds she could never flower.
Dark earth blotted the sky in a world upturned
Where our freedoms were left unsecured
To be bought and sold to the highest bidder:
The stakes were too high not to reconsider.
And with a volley of voices our wave arose
To wash away such madness and depose.

Appointing an Anchor
@mmxxpoet

Standing.

In front of a mirror,

Gazing at the sight of a body that she barely recognizes

Touching few strands of hair left on her head.

Breathing slowly, she gathers courage.

With her lifeless fingers she undresses her pink gown

The sight petrifies her, and she turns her face around

Her heart bleeds and she...

she wishes it was just a bad dream,

A nightmare.

The war she fought took away her soul.

She felt naked, shamed, ruined, uncertain.

She felt Unloved,

She was terrified.

But

Deep somewhere, inside her

A mother, a daughter, a wife, a sister, a warrior

Shakes her inside out

And

Screams,

Accept the tragedy that has occurred and fight with every ounce of

bravery, which is left in your

frailed frame.

Since you have to.

Since You have to.

With every bit of strength left in her she raised her head up looked in

the mirror again,

Smiled and whispered,

There are still lots of battles to encounter

But

There are loads n loads of courage reserves still left inside me.

"there is still a lot of fight left in me"

86

You stand in front of me.

Full of imperfections, pain, scars.

With Your teary red eyes.

You stand in front of me

wrecked, intoxicated.

You seem exhausted, restless.

There are new wounds, they weren't there last time you visited.

I see you bleeding.

I know why you're here.

You want me to hold you, accept you.

Me to protect you

Befriend you

You just want to be embraced.

I know. Hesitating or terrified

As always, I close my eyes, wishing for you to leave.

My heart feels like it will explode.

While praying for you to disappear.

I sense something on my face.

I open my eyes, and to my surprise tears flooded down

I look up, at you

You stand still

In the mirror, waiting for me to embrace you.

@ayesha._.afzal

Your words,

Just a sentence.

Caused a laughing soul to burst into tears.

Your expressions,

The faces you made,

The way you rolled your eyes.

Caused a joyful soul to lose its essence.

Your smirk

Flew away her dream

Nothing was left in her to beat.

Astonishing,

Isn't it?

That now,

You the "Society"

Just sits back and wonders

How come she drowned in devastation?

With no way back.

@ayesha._.afzal

There's enough drags
left on this city
like a cheap cigarette
and you can't
kick the habit.
Streetlights
illuminate the woeful drunks
while the common folk
sleep
and the cars speak
an angry language
sounds of speakers
and bass shaking
the ground beneath
lonesome shoes
of vagabonds.
It's at this hour
when the fog from
dusted off bibles
makes you squint
to see the good from the bad
or at least those lost
souls in transition.
Born again like the
sun over the South Shore.

Or for the hopeless,
the pesky weed
peeking through the
cement cracks.
When the new beginning
is all over
and the town is covered
with black
maybe the good word
will have spread
to the downtrodden
night dwellers
and there will be
a few more
winos and buggards
sleeping soundly
as they let
the devil's hour
pass.

@ryanpoetry

I wish I had words to make you
stumble through the shadows
of your dreams
and see the light
at the end of the tunnel.

I wish I lived in Brooklyn
so I could see trees
growing through cracks.

I wish that for every moment
in my head
there was a lifetime
with her instead
because the opposite has broken
my internal clock
the shock rocking me to sleep
as I question the
reality of time.

I wish that wishes
grew in orchards
so I could have
an apple a day
to keep the uncertainty away.

I'd move to the countryside and
pick up spoiled fruit
because I don't prescribe to the
concept that a few bad apples
can ruin the bunch.

But if I ever found
a magic lamp
I'd probably be too shy
to wipe away the dust
its history too deep and memories
too robust
and my hopes and desires
are not worth the fuss.
The genie would roll his eyes
as he grants my
pathetic demand
and he'd beg me to
wish away the other two
to escape the solitude
that he shared in my presence.

I'd watch Aladdin and
think of flying rugs
princesses marrying commoners
fools chasing love
hearts devoid of bitterness
and poets finding
the diamond in the rough.

With no need for the pen
and a mind at ease
I'd take my wishes
and set them free
guide you to the light
give you all of my fruit
some of it rotten
my imperfections in view
but this life, these words, these wishes
they have always been for you.

My Wish List
@ryanpoetry

your smile reaches your eyes
as you look into mine;
and for a split second,
i swear,
you almost saw me

@brady_poetry

tricking the mind

erase the manifesting voice of desire,
haunting choruses echo
"you're better than that"

i have myself fooled

until i take a glance;
a momentary relapse,
and feel the feeble facade
f r a c t u r e

i fall once again,
with no end in sight

tricking the heart

@brady_poetry

i stare at my reflection
and a stranger stares back

who is he?

most days i can't recognize myself at all

but i recall a time;

a time when the green grass stained
calloused feet
and the sun burned
feeble shoulders

the shoulders of a boy
so certain he could lift the entire world
as if he were atlas himself
always satisfied with that certain feeling
of fulfillment
that i lost so long ago

as his shoulders broadened

his horizons narrowed

and the world

he thought

he had secured in his hands

slipped through his fingers

he fell

and that boy

who had his future set

in the comforting certainty of stone

has since left my tiring grasp

and i am left

alone

@brady_poetry

I felt life in my veins. A soft feeling, almost like little sparks of light, almost like fireflies in a dark night. I breathed in the air and let it reach deeper than my lungs, realizing that we tend to chase experiences that will take our breath away, forgetting to find the moments that will remind us to breathe again. The sky was filled with little diamonds, the world being a ball filled with hope. Some turn to parties to get them high on life, but all I need is a clear summer night or a snowy evening in order to feel alive. The world felt silent yet filled with sound, and I felt whole, yet incomplete. There's a beauty in feeling human. A beauty in staring far off into the sky, until you see that part where it seems to slope downwards, creating an image of a globe. The part where the blue sky seems to touch the sea and the green hill seems to touch the white clouds. Some like to chase substances to make them feel alive, but I'd rather stare at the world and rediscover life. While they're at parties getting drunk on the dance floor, I'd rather dance in the sand and laugh from pure joy. We're all living in the same world yet on different wavelengths, just trying to enjoy our lives and make it last. We all have moments that make us glad to be alive; we all have moments that make us feel life.

@inkfrommysoul

Find what fills your heart with joy. What makes it light up brighter than the Northern Lights. What makes it feel like it's flying higher than the clouds. I close my eyes and I see cities I've never yet danced upon in countries I've never yet traveled to. I see mountains and breathtaking views, I see cobblestone streets in Europe in the rain. I see winter nights that are filled with warmth, as well as accomplishments and personal growth.
Sometimes we love to have everything planned out, but maybe life isn't meant to be planned. Maybe life is meant to be lived with the complete and utter belief that great things will come when they're meant to. Lived with the belief that everything will happen in its beautiful way, but all we need to do is find those things that fill us with joy.

@inkfrommysoul

Some look for darkness in pretty colors, others, colors in
black darkness,
Saying dreams are but a fantasy, while others make it
their reality,
Some live life to gain wealth, others live life to give from
themselves,
Viewing life as a time to plant a seed, others just
keeping up with society.

So how can we judge as though we know, when we all
live in our own minds?
Making time count in our own ways, yet we count the
times when another strays,
We discuss lives like storybooks, yet fight to have our
own personal voice,
See, we all live lives beneath the surface, in the same
world but with a different purpose.

@inkfrommysoul

I've become intoxicated with the idea of death
and its empty promises— the way it whispers
invitingly in my ear as I fall asleep
and caresses my spine with the tips of its
lengthy fingers— only to be awoken moments
later and greeted by life with tear-filled eyes and
false illusions,
Death owes me an apology for the way it
kills an already dead thing, for the way it
promised a promise it couldn't keep,
for the way it knocked the wind
out of my crumbling body.
If death were human, I already decided it'd be
a man— slow to come and quick to leave with
a stinger the size of his ego and a mouth that
drips venom with every word he speaks.
I thought I wanted death,
but now it is death that wants me.

Death's Promises
@ashleymilixza_

Should I have a daughter, I will warn her about
the hurricane to come,
the tornado storming to sweep her whole,
the flood she'll drown in if she doesn't seek shelter.
I'll tell her not to be the sun.
"Yes, you're beautiful."
"Yes, you're bright."
"Absolutely, the whole room
stops and stares cause you are
a walking light in a world of pain,
but this is not all I want you to be."
I'll warn her about the boy with his eyes
darker than the cloud above him.
He will want her to be his sun.
He will want her to die,
so that he may awaken back to life.
"This is not love," I'll tell her.
If she is anything like her mother,
she won't listen.
She'll want to fix him.

But I'll tell her,

"You are not a tool in his shed,

You are not a miracle worker,

and what sits between your thighs

is not the pathway to your heart."

"He will have to spend years searching

for the galaxies in your eyes

and decades learning the curves of your smile

because it is so simple to learn the curves of your body

& believe me, he knows them all

without you even undressed."

"But to learn the curves of your smile

is to learn what makes you happy.

Not what makes you unfold for him,

but what makes you laugh with him."

Should I have a daughter,

I'll warn her how easy it is

to glue someone's broken pieces together

without gluing back oneself

& I'll beg her, *please don't.*

Should I have a Daughter
@ashleymilixza_

You always spoke of buying
a house in the future
somewhere in the suburbs
far away from the city that made you.
Made us.
You wanted a backyard
with fresh green grass
and a fence taller than the
one you put up so that I
can't get in.
I wanted to live in a studio
somewhere in the city
that made you and I.
In this city,
we are together.
In that house,
we are not.

The City That Made Us
@ashleymilixza_

Probably because I kept thinking about her in that other movie with Paul
Rudd I can't remember the name of

this is how I start the conversation / this is how I say the word 'crush' and
look you in the eye / I mean / it's not my most pathetic moment ever /
definitely, maybe / but now you won't stop talking about that one film
where Jennifer Garner realises she loved the Hulk all along / I want to
say / shut up! / I'm right here! / but instead I punch your arm and point
out he wasn't the hulk just then / whatever whatever / something's gotta
give / right? / you grin at your phone / and I imagine for a moment that
you're looking at my new profile picture and thinking I look pretty in
pink / rather than pulling up Jackie Chan's IMDb page to prove I was
wrong about him having a cameo in the second, no-first, Bridget Jones
movie / come on you fool / say anything! / minus any spoilers for the
third one / tell me you feel it too / I don't mean electricity (which despite
what you say is as overrated as any Nicholas Sparks film) / I'm talking
about that feeling you get when something momentous is about to
happen / and you think to yourself / 'now?' / and the universe answers
yes / I think we could be good together / which is to mean all my space
metaphors orbit around you / and the two ticks next to my messages got
me thinking that perhaps blue really is the warmest colour / oh man /
I haven' been this misty-eyed since Patrick sang to Kat using a school
band / I'm not saying love exactly / but I am squeezing your initials into
margins without context / so yeah, I reckon I could get there / that is / in
an au where my crush actually likes me back / whatever whatever / I can
sit here and pretend that this isn't my most pathetic moment ever / that
I know all the scenes you're talking about from The Great Gatsby that
never made it into the film / that I'm totally okay pretending / as you sit
close next to me / completely and utterly / clueless.

n.k

Alicia Silverstone really creeped me out in that movie'
@flxw.d

103

I tried calling but I think ur phone is on silent / anyway

I did another one of those buzzfeed quizzes / about what type of bread I am /I got sourdough / which is kind of embarrassing but

tbh I can kinda see it / what do u think?

this is a sleepy town / and I lie awake at the idea that I do not exist outside its morning breath /

my loneliness is a door-to-door salesman / always coming away empty-handed /

b honest / do I disgust u? /

let me turn down the self-pity / I kno how to b useful /

I can turn my unsent messages into micro-poems 4 the masses / meaning

if I can't get a text back can I at least get an instagram like? lol .

#instapoets #poems #f4f #britneyspears

n.k

when britney spears said my loneliness is killing me
@flxw.d

so it's summer

and I cannot unclench my teeth

for more than a few seconds at a time.

August is a hot-headed fool and I see

my reflection in his sweaty palms.

do you miss me yet? I drive myself to the beach

and sacrifice seawater breath.

Dream of my head under the waves and

you waving goodbye.

In the daytime it seems like everything is bathed in light

& I am both jealous and afraid.

watching the sun set takes forever but

I need to know that there is some order to how things happen.

I miss you something rotten.

In weather like this dehydration will get to me faster.

Does your mouth dry up saying my name?

You do not have to answer. It's too warm to even move.

Stand out in the sun for too long and your skin starts to peel.

Saying your name for too long starts to pull it apart.

The heat cannot handle this

many layers.

Perhaps I never stood a chance.

n.k

August Fool
@flxw.d

I watch you as you
spill blood every day
to build a temporary shelter
from wolves that are drawn to
the smell of flesh
while you should be chasing them
with a torch and flames,
for you are supposed to be
a hunter, not prey.

@ta_poetess

I tried to unsheath claws
and show my teeth,
but it seems that
bravery requires elegance
and the lack of fear.

@ta_poetess

And maybe that's what endings are all about:
having nothing else to say and letting silence
sneak where love never could.

@ta_poetess

Some days
I just wish I could give it a name:
this darkness inhabiting my veins.
so that people wouldn't stare or
Turn away.
When the spiral closes in and I
no longer know what to do or say.
Some days
I just wish there could be a label:
she's damaged, but that is okay.

@citylightsandsunbeams

You ask me how it makes me feel
oh, where do I begin?
when everything just feels so black
and you are at the verge of giving in
Explain to me the silence's sound
casting shadows on the ground
when the moon has lost its magic light
and the sun but blinds your sight
When you ache for something, anything
Tender
'cause you're standing on the sharp edge of
Surrender
to those destructive arms
Tell me, do you not hear the alarms?

@citylightsandsunbeams

I try to move on

Like chasing flies in my apartment:

Buzzingly present.

Always out of reach.

and I know if I

one day catch them

They'll leave a trace

(of blood)

Just like these memories

(of you).

@citylightsandsunbeams

You were the boxer and I

The punching bag.

which is to say;

Your knuckles are bleeding

My soul is bruised.

@citylightsandsunbeams

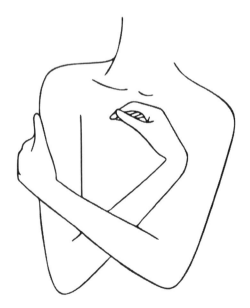

I count it a privilege to carry these bones;

do you know how often

I feel I cannot bear the day upon my back,

rise with the sun each morning,

anchor patience in the harbor of ribs so near to my heart's home.

Do you realize we are wonders

gifted laughing lungs,

bending to our own breezes

while withstanding everyone else's.

Please, oh, please whisper to me surely

that you know

what it is

to forget to thank your bones

and watch them save you anyway.

Privilege

@pocketfulofpoems

I'll meet you in a poem some day

Under this vagabond sky.

Orion will unbuckle his belt,

And all the stars will fall around the universe of our almosts,

Scattering our yesterdays into an uncharted stretch of constellations and skin.

All of this to say, I am waiting for you.

All of this to say, (if you must), take your time.

All of This to Say

@pocketfulofpoems

I want to tell you
often
like August rain
that you are so brave
for living in that ferocious way
that you do;
that you are softer than snapdragons,
heartbreakingly soft,
the kind of soft that stays.

Like August Rain
@pocketfulofpoems

I don't always know
the best way to live,
but for now?
To stumble across
this green, wide earth
with kind hands
is enough.

Enough
@pocketfulofpoems

Tepid, cool, the air

Stings my face with loneliness,

Slicks the stalks of my hair

Gypsies, Calypso-

and Sea Nymphs dance,

'Round a Pagan Fire,

Forever, in the dark air

Crazy, wicked wind,

Chills the mortal coil,

Like an arctic tide

Kissed by celestial,

cold, White Light

and Dead Men swear,

In the Space between spaces,

where a Virgin Maiden,

Drapes her bosom

in Twilight,

when the Moon passes,

'Neath her Misty Veil

-wolves bay,

Towards their reflection,

in the speckled,

Ebony ocean

where fevered dreams,

Trickle over

and become

Apparent,

as their

Wayward path

is

Pale

-and swim,

through Amber Spotlights,

down Urban Avenues,

and lie fair-

Under the Evanescent,

exhalation

of Ancient, elemental-

Breath, that

forever,

forever,

Slumbers,

Here.

Wild,

is the Night.

Wild is the Night

@johnleonmon

When soft tears do flow

As winds of melody are winding

It's not from pangs of tonality

Star-crossed harmonies

Pierce the flesh

Without bleeding

Harp strings bend

To abstract, yet

Universal understandings

Without inconsiderate

Confounding

Thundering rhythmic

Sacred geometry

Are but blameless witness

To the crime of time

And it's passing without

Empathy

The moving movement

Of sonic vibrancy

Are but dull reminders

Of sharp memories

But music never hurt,

No body

Music Never Hurt
@ johnleonmon

These
desperate hours
Are reckless muses
That pry
the decayed
and fragile
mind

as with Anemone
Death springs
Rebirth-
Cognizance, stricken
bled
on thoughts,
Dormant; fed,
as fine compost
and like poor Adonis,
Divine envy
smites the Revelator
For
*"Beauty is truth,
Truth, beauty"
a secret
Immortality keeps

And so,
the fire wielding
Prometheus
be forever
Damned,
and
Aphrodite
Weeps

*Ode on a Grecian Urn
by John Keats

-*Aphrodite Weeps*
@ johnleonmon

The fates of chance,

That our sweet glances,

Should ripen,

ferment,

or barely last

-and you'll never see me,

as sweet as then

Our first impasses

And my eyes,

Shall never not reflect,

The ghosts of our past

It either intoxicates

with age,

or blackens on the vine

But then,

'Tis twice as sweet,

Thrice divine

-or it passes,

through intermittent,

periods of bitterness, ravaged,

With the briefest periods,

of bitter sweetness

I don't know how,

but the grapes have soured,

It's bitter now.

Black on the Vine
@ johnleonmon

i voyaged the world
through the words
i have read.
searching for realities
that did not exist.
each day that went by,
i ruthlessly consumed from
a mouth I did not possess.
each sentence I spoke, I found it hard to believe.
the pretence was gluttonous.
it was a blessing when i split in two,
and a thousand books fell out of my head.
what was left was a paperback,
the contents familiar,
and the authors name was my own.

@fishahpoetry

i followed the moon and it lead me
to the face of an unborn flower.
i knew then, that this was my vocation.
as i laid my hands on to the earth,
it drew me close to its scent,
and i listened,
as my floral heart was being nurtured.
this was my voice, my rewilding.
this is where my aching feet had learned how to grow.

@fishahpoetry

years had passed by, before i even knew the moonrise
i felt as old as the sky and yet as young as the first drop of rain.
and as i tread through the living world of people and laughter,
i feel a life that pulses through the heart, like the river to a solitary stream.
i catch each breath of the shifting sun,
and it teaches me that everything i know can change.
why is it, that i did not know i was unhappy,
until i no longer was?

@fishahpoetry

i scatter my darkest thoughts into the sky.
i watch as they silently weave themselves
through the stars before returning to me,
faintly aglow.
i try to make sense of it all,
and have come to the conclusion,
that this shadow,
this river of grey beneath my skin,
is only a stepping stone.
a crossing,
a moment in time,
a brief encounter
an old memory,
just watching and
silently waiting for me to walk by.

@fishahpoetry

She kicked
up the dust,
and danced among
decayed leaves.

Messages written
by her hand,
were found in the
most terrific storms,
and in calm nights.

Picking up
all of the fallen things
was her calling.

There was nothing
she loved more
than watching the ascent.

Something About Joy
@sara_kelly_poetry

An immovable object,
set in stone.
She is the rock,
the Earth,
solid ground.

A heart easily moved,
flows like water.
Warm to the touch,
yet refreshing in a way
that one doesn't encounter
often, in a world this cold.

With wild curls
and a sarcastic laugh,
she is the sun,
and she will always
be the breeze.

Breeze
@sara_kelly_poetry

Once, she was a steady burn,
and a pretty please.
Nothing more
than a whisper
in a world full of
screams.
She found that
a flickering candle
was all she would
need to be.
All along, she
had been afraid
of the dark,
needlessly.

Candle
@sara_kelly_poetry

I have crossed a thousand seas to find you
Nestled in the sky so blue,
Spoken words of dreams incarnate,
Timeless letters from which to choose.
I have met you a thousand lifetimes before
And we speak with a knowing, no words could say
I know that even when our physical bodies
Have left one another,
Our souls have never parted ways.

Atlantis...
@etherealimaginings

Where my heart goes
Poetry flows,
This cycle I could never halt,
And when my eyes see
The aliveness of this dream,
In my mind there opens a vault
I am the molten lava burning down the hillside
The stone that skips across seas
The river that flows
Down the mountain that knows
That nothing is ever as it seems
Or is it exactly?
The point where opposite sides connect
In-between the flip of a coin
The hesitant stare
Of a stranger who cares
The tangling of vines in the loin
The contracting breath
The last, and first, left
And the closing of fog shrouded eyes,
I bid you hello, good morning and goodnight
Sleep well, good riddance, goodbye.

Where I Am...
@etherealimaginings

If all is but a reflection
Then your eyes reflect the sea
And the river that flows
Is the bridge of your nose
Your eyes, the flowers and trees.
And I am the moon floating gently,
Watching with care from above
And the world keeps on turning
The embers still burning
An endless culmination,
Of love.

SeaNoEvil...
@etherealimaginings

My love,

Have you ever heard the wind cry?

Not in isolation

But rather

In ravishing relation

With the rest of the world

With the universe

Unbound

I hear it howl and it sounds

Like infinity

I am in a perennial state

Of reverie

Mesmeric Tears

@katarinaannepoetry

Lilac lullabies

Whisper sweet symphonies

To the skies of tomorrow

Tucking in all of our yesterdays

And kissing the moon goodnight

Unborn thoughts linger

Amongst a sea of

So many souls

Who will rise again with the sun

And dwell upon the earth as one

Goodnight Universe

@katarinaannepoetry

Shedding the layers of lies
I have absorbed over time
Only to find that the truth
Has been beneath them all the while
My poetry whispers within me
Consistently
Unraveling my thoughts
And yet piecing them together
The ego is dissipating
But whether or not it disappears
I am here
I am breathing
And that is enough

Ego Vs. Consciousness
@katarinaannepoetry

Can you hear it?

The breath of the universe

I breathe and suddenly

We are synchronized

We are one

I come undone and I realize

That I am both everything and nothing

All at once

Interconnection

@katarinaannepoetry

if you recognize yourself in my lines
it's because i tenderly placed
your face.
your hands.
& your lips.

@layla.poetry

i've always loved dedication pages

tore them out gently

stacked them

and read your name on every line

@layla.poetry

it will be worth it

even if you break my heart & step on the pieces

twirl on my ashes &

laugh

i will rise from the fire

ready to be hurt by you

with my phoenix heart

@layla.poetry

I have seen the old man sitting in the park
watching the pond fill with peach blossom.

The widow-man knows the Secret,
his scarlet necktie is a remembrance of sex –
his white hair the soft down in a sparrow's nest.

Such simplicity falls to earth with the blossom.
We are like the carp on the surface of the pond:
mouths open, we swallow each morsel of life.

Will it take until my hair turns silver to find
that my heart was never broken? Michael,
you yourself are the Dragon's Gate, all Heaven
and Earth is within you. The pink snow

falling through the fruit trees. The Chinese carp
in their shallow pool, the widower
and the sparrow weaving her little nest.

Even the tears which well in the sage's eyes
is the calling from a joy that never left you.

Dragon's Gate
@vitruviuspoetry

Walking on the street,
pattering of raindrops
on my cheeks.
I looked up to the sky
through my hazel eyes.
Exquisite it looks,
golden drops under
the street light.
I looked back to the city.
All flashy neon lights,
alluring soul's flight.
Buildings so high
catching one's sight.
Not my intention anymore,
I'm the solivagant soul.
Finding my home
long lost.
On this street once
I walked on
to my only home.

@fahmidapoetry

When pain arrives,

let it come

put it on paper.

burn it

smash it

stab it.

Make it realise

it has arrived

at the wrong door.

Your heart is home for

Kindness

Forgiveness

and love.

And not for pain

to accommodate.

It has to leave.

@fahmidapoetry

I like your face this way: half-covered in shadow,
the repose of your hip touched by the hand of twilight.
Let the sickle moon conquer the sighing dusk.

And so, the moon rises an hour later each night.
The new white moon of your body, the red full moon
of your lips: the black moon, sighing with your kiss.

You are caught in the pale basket of dawn
for beauty adorns herself in the lustre of a pearl
and in the sighing death of this night.

A Secret I Whispered to the Moon
@vitruviuspoetry

Perhaps it was your silence
that made me settle here...

Here, not among the willow
or in the boughs of the ancient Oaks,
nor upon the frozen pond,
but here in the rose-bed
where your voice sounds
like a lullaby of a thousand silences –
into those silences: I pour myself.

Your rose is an urn.

The moon hangs overhead.
Winter walks wearily over the lawn,
his footsteps crunch
into the apple-white snow.
November shakes the last petals
from the rose tree
and a white silence falls over the land
and everywhere I look is gleaming.

The dingle sleeps in the fold of a duvet
and the farmhouses doze in the valley.
The animals are tucked away in their burrows
and the birds asleep in their nests.
This evening the hills are covered in duck down.
We tumble: you and I, two feathers from one wing.
My ashes linger on your fallen lips
and I nourish your leaves.

So, the snow swirls

around like a congress of ghosts,

its powder forever impalpable.

The pines whisper to me

from faraway places,

they tell me of their deep stillnesses

and sometimes their restlessness.

When silence breaks open your flower,

we twirl around the garden

in a snowstorm of petals –

and you sing your lullaby

and it is perfect,

like a thousand years of silence.

Tonight, we will leave no tracks in the moonlight,

death and life melt into the other as if our lives

were like the symmetry of snowflakes.

The Rose Bed

@vitruviuspoetry

my rosebush makes me blush / her canes have grown wild / reached out past the fence / she drops petals and leaves / until she stands bare / unashamedly naked / not caring if the neighbors stare / nonplussed by my red cheeks and raised clippers / she sinks her roots deeper / drinks in the rain / soaks up the sun // this is her season / her rest before the bloom / i tuck my shears away / some things should not be pruned

Flutterbye

@iamcheriscott

i acted like cleaning the patio / and rearranging furniture / around a
new fire pit / would keep our hearts from bleeding out // you were the
only honest one / asking / should i put out five chairs / or four

Pretending

@ iamcheriscott

love is energy / in me / in you / to the far ends of the earth and beyond // it can't be flipped on like a light switch / caught by a panel in the sun / or created by windmills on a hill // the power grid of love is smiles and hellos / undivided attention / letting people move at their own pace // apologies / forgiveness / commitment / care // love spreads in the living of it / in the giving / it is multiplied / magnified / electrified

Plugged In
@iamcheriscott

you touched this heart
with your gentle hands
wrapping your fingers
around it. how foolish,
i thought you were
claiming it as yours.
you were preparing
to rip it out.

heart
@sabinalaurapoetry

i said goodbye

with the wind in my hair

as it scratched at the surface

of what we became.

the storm rages on

now you're not there

but since then i've grown

to love the rain.

storm chaser

@sabinalaurapoetry

there's a war
between my heart
and head
and i can't sleep
these 4am thoughts
are too deep
and tearing me apart.

4am thoughts
@sabinalaurapoetry

What else

A smitten patch of Late love or

Fried bruises on table to the coffee mug

I open in vintage morning

A fresh colour resurrect

Bring me

mint brook in a kerosene Bowl

Pad these crescent voids

Fruit of aged tongue.

Like a blueprint to my blonde Lip. Now taste some tooth and smile.

Let Go

Cold cigarettes

smoke an old book instead

A sweetheart in plural wisdom

Breathe of A day

somewhere down the orange trees

Shuffling

Like children of the sun stitching clouds of blue.

A rest prayer consoling

sleep

You may Now

Calcimining quilted Poems

a Moon in peace.

Routine

@ecstatic_muse

A digit of grief
Incomprehensive of any utterance
Meaning, maybe some blue shadow of the past

Buried sonnets in pages
folded along the lip of this diary
Waiting, waiting for a lover's Call -

Acoustic, a rosewater fluency it possesses
Still
I confirm no images

Old terraces or half broken tea plates
Oscillations of burnt kisses
pulsating this velvet mouth
But no taste it sounds

For I am kindly a sold word
No remains in me
Of your modest toes, surrounding
windowsills
lay a parchment of this floor
across my saturn skin

And the dying leaves
chanting the same seasons
to these scars, sour green
Churning again to turn a blank page

@ecstatic_muse

A month slips satin
Off my room
Once more these clean words
of no tongue-
Inside my head they grow songs
of lemon dots and
Melancholy fingers moving like rabbit
Across my crispy hair

A handfull giggle

A toothsome gospel to my lonely nights

Walls peach, still in place
and moving tanned
I am quite attracted to late sun and sweet coffees now

Waving butterflies
Like young lovers cuddling
This mouth to a new season
opens my heart
Like a newborn letter
I smell of earth again

October
@ecstatic_muse

You are struggling,

you are battling with your own self.

This immense pain you are in is meant to leave soon.

Let the waves of emotions pour out,

let the pain escape.

Your spines are never meant to carry them.

You make yourself look like wrecked street

in curfew-imposed city, but you should know your worth.

Your heart is a temple

and the only pilgrims with pure intentions could enter it.

You have fields of sunflowers on your skin

blooming out of every cracks and crevices; ready to be harvest

and the next batch to come and so on.

How could you think of giving up? when the sun and the moon

and all the rains have circled you to grow wildly.

My dear you were created out of universe.

The galaxies rest on your lashes and stardust sprinkled on your

hair and your body has a glimmer of the moon.

How could you not shine?

You are anything and everything you wanted to be,

let yourself shine like a star.

Know Your Worth
@fahmidapoetry

ACKNOWLEDGMENTS

To all of the poets who contributed to this anthology:

Taylor, Jess, Anne, Kaitlyn, Marissa, Tisha, Claire, Grace, Ashley, Shylee, Georgina, Artisan, Kirstan, Miriam, Eliza, Elise, Elizabeth, Cicero, Emmi, Mathew, Camden, Molly, Navi, Audra, Melanie, Ayesha, Ryan, Brady, Shevy, Ashley, n.k, Soul Writing, Alyssa, John, Fehmida, Sara, Balladine, Katarina, Layla, Michael, Cheri, Sabina, Fahmida, and Sailani.

To the thousands of poets who submitted to be a part of this anthology and were not chosen: keep submitting and keep creating.

Thank you.

Molly Wolchansky, founder of Augie's Bookshelf

@augiesbookshelf on Instagram

Contact submissions@augiesbookshelf.com if you would like us to contact one of the poets in the book in regards to features and publications.

Printed in Great Britain
by Amazon